DOUBLE EDGED WORDS

BY

DELUKE MUWANIGWA

A collection of poetry

By Deluke Muwanigwa

ISBN:
Hardbound-978-621-470-653-2
MOBI/KINDLE-978-621-470-654-9
Softbound/Paperback-978-621-470-655-6

Published by:
Poetry Planet Book Publishing House
Rosario, Pozorrubio, Pangasinan, Philip-pines
Contact Number: 09554960094
Email: maritesritumalta@gmail.com

ACKNOWLEDGMENTS

I would like to thank my wife, Barbara, whom I used as a bouncing board for many of my poems, my son Dananayi for helping with formatting stuff and generally helping where my computer knowledge was obsolete. My daughter, Mudiwa Nathasia, for assisting with various foreign currency payments for software.

My indefatigable professional friend, Engineer Trust Chifamba. Engineers Michael Mawire, Nashon Msumba and Shepherd Chipindu . They supported my first self-published book "Mbiresaurus" and encouraged me to keep going

And, of course, to my Publishers and Printers, a big thank you to all.

Deluke Muwanigwa. C. 2023

PREFACE

Double Edged Words.

The title of this book is derived directly from one the poems by the same name.

Poetry has the power to evoke different emotions in different individuals depending on many factors, some of which are cultural experiences, life experiences, personality etc.

Some words are like double edged swords; double edged words; meaning one thing, but implying another.

This book, which I hope readers will enjoy, is hopefully the eighth of many. As long as I live, I will always have an opinion and I enjoy expressing myself in poetry.

I hope you enjoy this collection of poetry.

.

Deluke Muwanigwa. C. 2023

TABLE OF CONTENTS

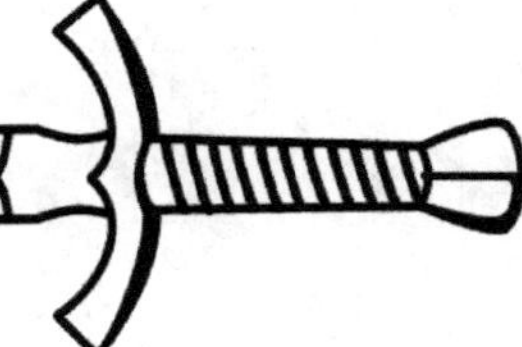

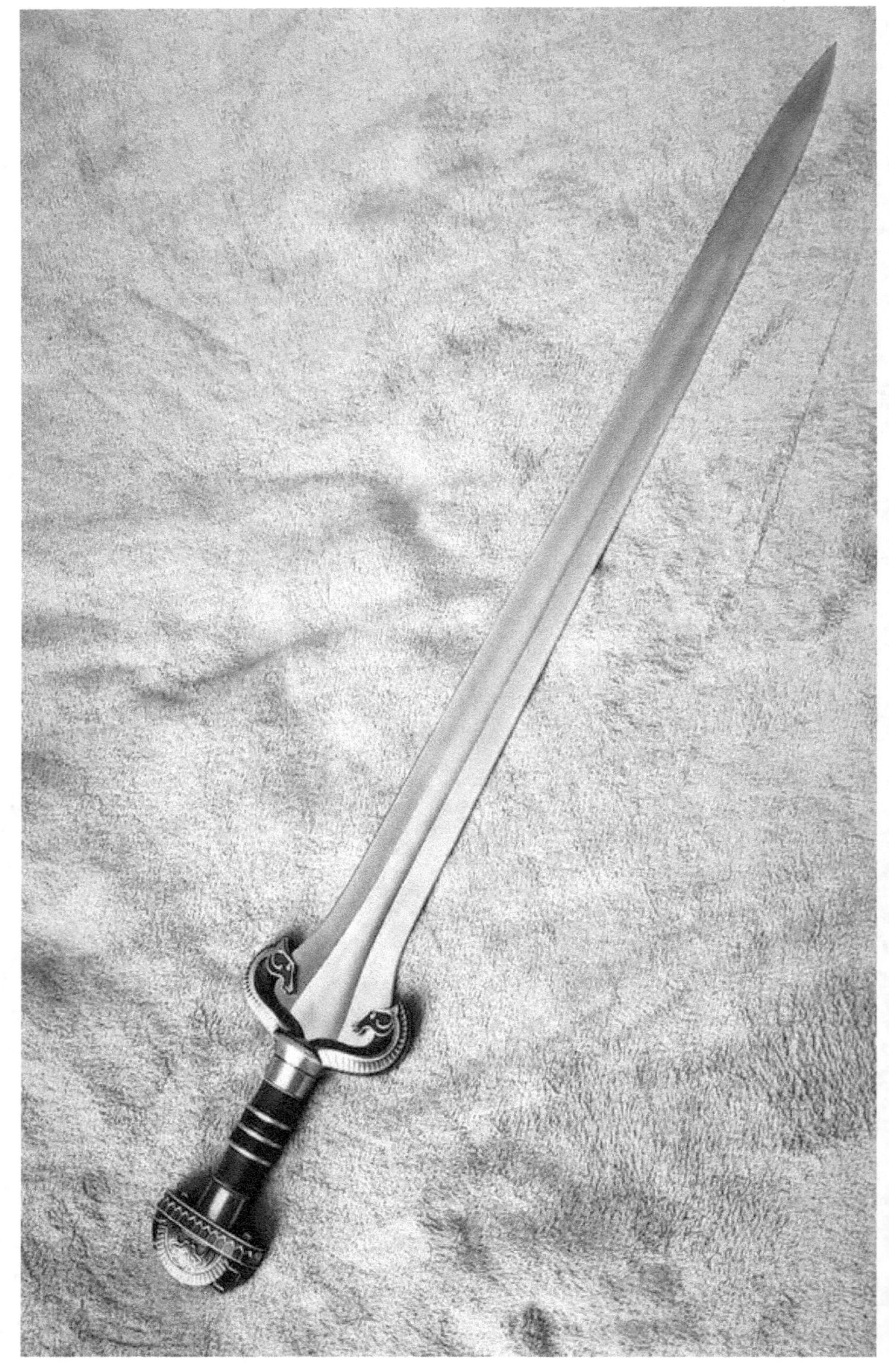

SKIES BRAWL

The heavens have guttural conversations
Hidden behind dark swirling curtains
Deep voices sounding agitated
Someone up there ends up crying
Gallons upon gallons of tears coming down.

We love it when the gods fight behind dark shrouds
We on the ground celebrate their bad moods
That's the time we grow food
Sometimes, though, the fighting gets nasty
And sparks of mega anger hit the ground violently

We lose lives
Livestock
Homes
And homesteads.

What can we do when the gods are crazy?
No use being lazy
We make merry while they fight
Our elation grows.
When Skies Brawl.

EXTRA HIGH TENSION

I am an Extra High-Tension wire
Four hundred and forty thousand Volts.
Someone will be shocked
When the short happens
When I discharge
Emotions
Apprehension
Tension
Unexpectedly.

Standing stoic
A steel pylon for years
Absorbing the shocks
Of deadly charges
For other's
Mania
Depression
Meltdowns
Steadfastly

The rust is setting in
Fatigue bearing down
Insulation failing
Life cycle ending
Time is nigh for
Exploding
Breaking down
Imploding
Anytime soon.

IS A WINNER A SINNER?

Is a winner a sinner?
A winner is not necessarily a sinner
As a sinner is not necessarily a swimmer
Because a sinner maybe a swimmer
And still be a winner
There is a winner
And there is a sinner
The distinction gets thinner
For a beginner
Like a swimmer
Who is a schemer
Snorting thinners
Pretending to be a dreamer
When they are just a performer
A screamer
Enhancer
Doper
Cheater
Sinner
Acting like a winner
It's quite an enigma
So, let's talk after dinner

AS IT IS

I am sitting on a dining room chair in my bedroom. I brought it in sometime back to watch TV because it was more comfortable for me. The sofa had the ignominy of inducing sleep once you sunk in it. To my left slightly behind me is the main window. Lace curtains and embroidered drapes drawn to the sides. My king size bed is next, the headboard hard up against the wall. A forlorn photo of my daughter when she was eight stuck on the wall just above the headboard.

At the foot of the bed is the bedroom sofa. On the settee, a cushion, my wife's dress, morning gown, handgrips for her physio and her cellphone. On the other wall a dressing table with an assortment of cosmetics. There is a pair of dumbbells on the dressing table, also for her physio and then a doorway to my man cave. A little dressing room full of daddy paraphernalia and the second bedroom window. Files on a wooden bookshelf with lyrics and poems I wrote since 2001. Thereon my poetry certificates and a laminated copy of a poem " Songs of Solomon" I wrote sometime back. On the floor, an exercise ball and my shoes strewn all over. In front of me, my modest dressing table and drawers for my socks, undies and plugs, sockets, screws and an assortment of hardware (men are strange).

Behind my dressing table the ensuite bathroom. Shower, water closet, wash hand basin and tub on the other wall. A door leads back to the bedroom and on the left of the door a fridge after which is a door leading in and out of the bedroom

To my right, as I sit, built in cupboards for my wife. Three of them. She is always giving away clothes in Zim Bags. Zimbabwe Bags. (Huge bags used by cross border travellers, most of whom are Zimbabweans, earning the bags the name,) but her cupboards are always full. Next to the built in cupboards, another stands alone chest of drawers with clothing. Next to me on the right, an OLED TV on a glass topped stand and a glass coffee table next to it to match. Welcome to my bedroom. As it is.

Any one for a visit?

TIME

The timing of time is independent
Wishing it to conform to a will is futile
Because time times itself to its own rhythm
Either you conform to its dictate or you lose.

The cliche, "time does not wait for anyone" is time worn
But, those who take it as a cliche
Well, they see stars timed out
Looking up, wishing on a star
In the wrong galaxy
Their destiny having moved on in time.

As early as yesterday we had a meeting penciled for 10am
At 10am a feeble message came in just in time
Letting us know the time of the meeting was now noon.
Realising the import of that which we wanted
The time wasted was granted
But even by midday they failed to arrive

Again, another timeout message
Further "delays due to unforeseen circumstances"
The meeting finally happened well past 2pm.
It was rushed
Program crushed
The conveners now more acutely aware of time
The sun beginning to shed its shine.

In time we will do a post-mortem of why we failed
And as usual the reason will never be nailed.

That, failure is ingrained in our wanton disregard of a thief
The one that taketh stealthily while you lumber and slumber
While you behave as if life owes you a living
It is thieving
Surreptitiously taking away opportunity
And we, failing as a community

We, a motley crew of failures
Like hapless sailors
Who failed to prepare the ship before the storm
Had it torn
In time
By time.

NIGHTMARES

There are things I want to say
Weighing heavily on my mind
Possibly write a poem
Before I lose it.

Unfortunately it seems,
Even in poetry
To write what is sitting on my mind
Words fail me

If I could I would
I would pluck beautiful airy words from the air
Pick the best aromatic flowers, turn them to words
Figments of my eloquence turning figs of imagination to verses

My vocabulary fails me
The colloquial worse
At best
My experiences will come alive in poesy

Whereas people watch sci-fi
I have lived it
I am in the middle of fiction
Except it's reality

So I went in search of words
To bring to life what I felt
What I saw
What I went through

Snippets will come alive in poetry
Disjointed
Seemingly unrelated components
Of nightmares

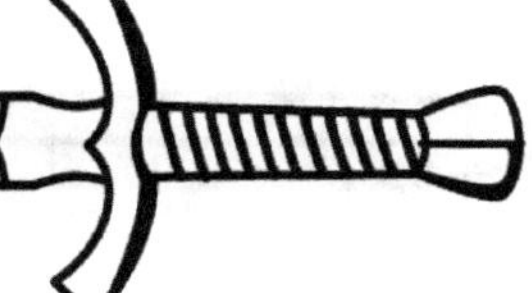

OBSESSIVE COMPULSIVE BEHAVIOUR

Grown adults are kids with this condition
The condition
They want it now ..like right now
Doesn't matter how....
The mind creating its own rendition
Of the justification for the immediacy
No amount of persuasion can temper down the tempo
Like a crazy nun married to the temple
Believing she is Mary the Virgin
When we all know she's just Mary the vegan.
Like all things lacking negative feedback
Contradictions fight back
Generosity to undeserving ones
At the same time sanctioning other nuns.
Believing in one's own delusions as the gospel truth
And seeking refuge in manufactured reality for truce
Many times leading to uncontrollable positive feedback
Leading to commission of mistakes
When the deck of cards crumbles
It is the beginning of troubles
Insomnia
Apnoea.
Depression
Expression
Of Obsessive compulsive behaviour.

TWERKING N' WORKING

I wrote a poem in a dream last night
Something to do with twerking n' working
A people living near the equator
The women beautifully full bodied
Dressed skimply in mini skirts
And nothing else other than a bodice
The men dressed in traditional attire
Animal skins covering their manliness
And nothing else other than beautiful native skin.

These people loving dancing
Twerking, twerking, twerking
Whenever they met it was a music and dance affair
No instruments
Clapping rhythms with hands
Drum beats the stomping of feet
Powerful voices carrying their epiphanies beyond the valleys and mountains

Ladies slightly bent over wriggling behinds
Twerking, twerking, twerking
Tweaking their cheeks from side to side
In simple harmonic motion
Men clapping in time to each tweaked twerk, stomping feet.

When they went to their fields they would dance and twerk until their fields were beautifully done
Out there in the sun
Having fun

Twerking, twerking, twerking
Working, working, working
Twerking n' working.
And I, too, in the dream
Twerking n' working till dawn.

RED AND WHITE ARMIES

Last night they attacked.

I woke up at three AM to the sound of pounding in my head quarter.

The overhead whirring of a flying master ship, itself dispatching little drones to attack me.

I could not see them but my army divisions used sophisticated sensors hidden in my breathing tunnels to detect them.

The red army was alerted by the signal's corps and in no time, there was mobilisation

The white army kept supplies to my pumping station and my intelligence headquarters head quartered.

The rising activity causing me to feel a little hot and claustrophobic.

Various incendiary was lobed down my ventilation ducts to try to flush the red army out. And initially I felt the might of the mites surrounding my nasal cavity. My body temperature went up and I woke up feverish.

My first reaction was to fear the dreaded biological agent of Chinese origin, but my red army had already been trained to deal with that. Twice they went for training and got inoculated against these bio agents. As long as the sub aqua team of the white army kept supplies moving, the red army would be ready.

When I woke up, my throat was dry. My nasal cavity was blocked and I was running a fever. Thoughts of the SARS-COV-2 battles crossed my mind, but I took comfort from knowing I was vaxxed and my trachea was not dry and I had no pain in my chest.

By late afternoon it turned out it was probably just dust mites from a ceiling fan which I run at night due to high temperatures. Thank God for my red and white blood cells for winning my battles. The red and white armies.

LIFE WITHIN LIFE

There is life within life
A situation taking its own trajectory
despite your best efforts
You lay in your bed, in your mind, playing videos of the day
And even venture into the enigmatic following day
When the time comes for reality
Your guess is as good as mine
Where reality takes you

People have spent billions
Used computer models to predict
Only to have reality wielding the upper hand.
Wars have been planned in minute detail
Invaders so sure of victory
Figs of their figment were not on the fig tree.

Diseases have been modelled
In the final analysis models mothballed
Because there is life within life
And within the new life there will be life and even a new life in the new
Adapt, adopt and be adept at whatever reality throws at you
Because there's life within life in this life.
Life within life

THE CEILING

Every evening I lie on my bed
Waiting for the silence to be just right
Giving space in my head
To recall things that come flooding in the night
I sleep with lights on
In case an emergency should arise
I must be quick on the phone
And quick to rise

The most entertaining screen in my bedroom is the ceiling
Lying on my back I scan it from corner to corner
It bears witness to things frightening and thrilling
A bullet hole of which I was not the causer.
Bearing testimony to some forbid history
Centre of the ceiling is a bigger hole
A ceiling fan now moved to the edge, so that is no mystery
The other hole the origin I do not know

If ceilings could talk, my bedroom ceiling would recite so many sonnets
Eight lines of good memories on top of six of sadness
Full of history and soulfulness
Maybe eight of strange stories of intrigue and six of madness
Of suicide attempts
And bed linens unkempt

DEPRESSION EXPRESSION

Drooping shoulders
Looking so down
Counting sheep
Lacking sleep
Bad mood
Hating food
Insomnia
And apnoea
Turn and toss
Memory loss
Cutting arm
Self harm
Suicide thoughts
Nerves taut
Death ideation
Self alienation
Loneliness
Emptiness
Hyper
Suddenly hypo
Withdrawn
Till dawn
Altered reality
Altered ability
Troubled silence
Doubled shyness
No friend
In the end
In the mind
Left behind

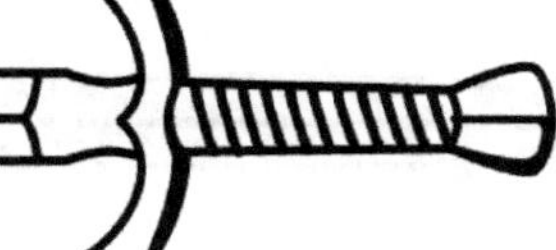

Pensive
Life expensive
In nightwear
Nightmares
During the day
Nothing to say
Desperation
Exasperation
Depression
Expression

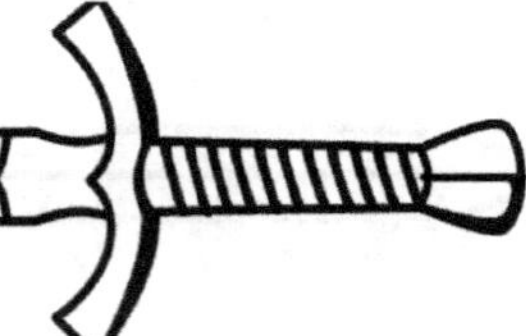

NINE METRES AWAY

Like I do more than once a day
I busied myself with the mechanics of survival
Gathered the requisite components
Stuff with mixes of carbon, hydrogen, oxygen, nitrogen in
complex bonds and many other elements
Water too
And gathered all by the jaw crusher
And initiated the processes

My last shift was at 18:00 and all looked normal
The raw materials looked pure
Balanced
Colourful even
And I set about loading my jaw crusher
Slowly and deliberately
Savouring my work
Put my plant on auto
And retired to bed.

3:00 was woken from my slumber
The ambient temperature way above normal
There was rumbling
Gurgling
Boiling and high pressure hissing
My process plant was in trouble
And I immediately set about making things right
Unclogged the system at the process's end.
Nine Metres Away.

THE BLACK HOLE

There is a black hole at the centre of our galaxy
The Milky Way
The mother of all gravitational masses
Fifty five million light years away
All the stars, planets and their moons of the solar system
are beholden to it
Billions of stars
Our little sun included
Our tiny earth included
Our little moon in the mix
Our lives included.

Relative to our earth the black hole has infinity mass
Enough power to keep billions of stars, planets and moons
in check
It creates new stars
The stars create and control their groups of planets and
moons
Rogue stars swallowed by the black hole
New ones squirted out
Giving life and death
And in similar ways
We get life
And we die

It will come to pass
After we cut down all trees
Deplete ozone
And our erstwhile friendly sun scorches us
We will all die

The sun will expand to singe the earth
After which the sun will die
We need to prepare for our rebirth
On another planet
Born again
Through The Black Hole

POEM AFTER POEM

I write poems from the heart
A heart with a regular heartbeat
and normal vital signs.

Even before the ink dries
I wonder whether what I write is right
Whether it will bring comfort to my troubled soul

The need for comfort brings melancholy
For, I wonder why I write to fight
those imaginary demons which trouble me

The ones casting an invisible shadow over all that I do
making me doubt myself
Making me ask myself
whether the ink brings out what I really think
or is just a cold comfort.

No answers come forth
and in the end I write for the sake of writing.
Poem after poem
Because I can.

SUNDAY BLUES

Sunday the fifth of December twenty twenty one.
I was in one of those meditative moods
As I am wont most Sundays for as long as I remember
There is always an aura of sadness on days like these
I have no explanation for the melancholy
Perhaps my lack of religiosity tugs at my emotional strings
Making me think of things
Beyond my locus of life
It's like
The religious music reaching me from a nearby church
Evokes sadness rather than happiness
Worse when I see the congregants on the street they look sad.
Haunted even.

Sunday the fifth of December
There was no exception
There was the hollow sound of an organ
Voices singing in discord floating above the depressing notes.
And I, in a meditative mood
Brooding
In need of a diversion
Something about which I had no aversion.
So I sent my mind beyond visual range
Scanning beyond the horizon
Meditating on the meaning of life to the music of a church organ
And soaking in my Sunday blues.

CHANCES

You know, chances are,
It is not a coincidence I exist
If it was it would also be
That by chance we all exist
That by chance the sun rises
And the moon by chance rises too

The heavens would hang above by chance
The wind blow by chance
The clouds hanging in the sky
The birds
And the seas
All by chance

Chances are we are part of creation.
And creation is a part of us.
When faced with a life and death situation
Give life a chance
Chances are you will also get a chance
If you know what I mean

DEAR LONELINESS

Dear loneliness
I want to acknowledge your loveliness
These days you are all I have
With you I have to brave
With humility
Feelings of futility

Gone are the days
When the wife of my youth used to say
Honey I love you
And I knew it was true

She said she was mine till the end of time
The end of her line
Came too soon
That afternoon

I cry, I wish, I hope
There was scope
To be together again
Her mortal train
Moved on
Leaving me on my own
With you, loneliness
And your loveliness

I embrace your grace
Face the race
To the terminal day
My death day

I shall leave your silence
Obey the science
Of life and death
Quietly join the earth
Leaving you, loneliness
And your loveliness

EXEUNT

Act one scene one
I said I am yours and you said you were mine
You were of a sober mind
And I, not under duress
That's what we thought
It was we and them
All those who did not take a vow
The vow that you and I took
We were intoxicated with elation

How is it then there were so many heartaches?
In the act
Behind the curtain
So much loneliness?
So many awkward positions?
So many I lost count?
Why is it then we wanted to take a bow?
Leave the stage?
Exit?

It used to make sense to fall in love
Carried away by whimsical naivety
The phantom called love came and left
Left unceremoniously
Through the back exit
Made its way out of our hearts
A masquerade hoisted on icy stilts
Stilts easily melting in the heat of betrayal
Foisted on us by a society full of theatrics
In a charade of a bogus ceremony

A ceremony sanctifying fiction

Your pledge to be mine,
To have and to hold
Has gone cold
I am yours and you are mine
That's what we thought
Now I am no longer sure

It used to make sense to be in love
Now it makes senses to fall by the wayside
To disembark at the quayside
In the dark
Society asleep
Instead of being stuck
In this act
Bow out
Exeunt.

MY X

A day will come to sail the
Boat whose fate will be even more
Cursed than the Titanic
Denying love is a mistake
Enraging my sane senses
Forcing me to leave you for
Good in a trip of no return
How did you really feel watching
In theatres and on TV
Juxtaposing our own lives
Knowing that time is now nigh
Loving you loving me now is
My main reason for breathing
Now you want to tell me that
Our love can no longer be
Please know that I cannot live
Quietly wishing on a star
Replaying what could have been
Sure it will never be
Today I journey without you
Unsure I will make it
Vowing never to love again
Without you my only love
X is not a letter I use
You can't be my X because my
Zeal for your love would kill me

MY SECRET ONION

If you peel my secret onion you will feel it
Acidic astringency hitting you smack on
Each peeling reeling with tasty secret secretions

Bipolar tastes in your molars
Dissociated identity disordered tastes in your buds ran-
domly ordered
Having so many shades and tastes when tested
Even fruit flies fail to intersect and dissect the secrets of my
onion bulb.
Let alone so called culinary connoisseurs.

Mine is not a shallot parading in a charade
It's the full round king of bulbs akin to humpty dumpty
Who sat on the wall
Came away with nothing
But holding secrets so dumb.

This is the story of my onion full of secret cations and ani-
ons at molecular level in each peel.
Each secret laden peel killing your appetite for secrets
Etched with secrets so deep it puts you to sleep,
As you remove a layer you are moved by the depth of the
effect,
An exquisite secret affecting your inquisitive nostrils and
eyes
And to think it has been like this all my adult life

I am the king of my secret onion
Keeping all these secrets despite opinions of minions

Armchair analysts whose ascetic attitudes are catalysts for depression.
Making life unappealing peeling my secrets without permission.

Touché!!

THE LIVING FREE

The living free
Are free
Living in a tree
Or out at sea

You see
There's no fee
Even for me
To be free

They are free
Want to be
Like a bee
Living free

They may struggle to feed
With a shortage of things
Not enough for their needs
As long as they have seeds

They won't lack for something
beans
Peas
Tea

The living free
Do you see
They feed from a tree

"The Giving Tree"

MY KIDS, MY SEEDS

Trees are leaving their leaves behind
Shedding the shed
Knowing fully well it's time to renew
Answering nature's overtures
To take a break
To hibernate

Looks are deceiving
Don't cry for the fallen leaf
Sent drifting in the wind
Excommunicated
The leaf having fallen
Will be food for pollen

I remember vividly the day of birth
My kids bundles of joy
A chubby boy
A charming little girl
Now I watch them drifting away
My kids are leaving me behind

To grow
I know
I am happy
Though sad
My seeds
Falling into the leaves I shed.

MY ROOTS

My heart traces its roots south of Zimbabwe, in Masvingo Province.
Five hundred kilometres by road
Three hundred and fifty kilometres as the crow flies.
The home of the Great Zimbabwe Ruins, from which my country derives its name.

My heart dons boots of nostalgia for the journey to my roots.
In that beautiful barren country of mountains and rich diamond pickings,
Alluvial gold and Asbestos too
My umbilical cord finds itself stuck in its history.

This is the land my forefathers fought for
Sometimes I ask myself what for
Why for?
Till I drive there.
It may be barren
But it's beautiful

There are scant rains
The little that falls drains
Channelled by mountains to huge dams.
Lakes and pans.
My kindred built their homes at the summit of a hill
Our hill
A place of spectacular views

To the north the imposing Makamba Mountain.

Legend has it that...but that will be for another day
To the south is the famed Border Munaka Mountain
Legend has it during the war regime forces never went beyond that "border"
The first name "Border" originates from that.

To the West at the foot of our hill is a diamond mine
The lights of the mine are the brightest beacon at night.
Where our hill and Makamba Mountain share their feet, there are a shopping centre, a school and my uncle's homestead

On an ant hill on the slope of our hill
Not far from our huts lies my father's grave
Killed in crossfire during the war
Lying next to him are the remains of his brother.

No matter how many droughts
No matter how many wars
My umbilical cord is stuck there
I am of the Karanga Tribe
Of the Fish Totem
The natives whose arses are stuck in this barren land.
Our ancestral land
My roots.

300 MILLION VOLTS

Small clouds bandied together
Shepherded by different gusts of winds
Trees sighed and sang
Shedding leaves as if to pay the ground self-serving taxes
Accumulating humus

The sun playing hide and seek
Behind darkening veils of water vapour
Itself coalescing into unsettled charged particles
Humans fretting at the unfolding deluge

A farmer told "Make hay while the sun shines"
Clouds make hail while the sun hides
A housewife scurrying to remove the almost dry washing
on the line
The clothes line tethered one end to a tall tree
And the dutiful woman not able to feel 300 million volts

Under the tree
Under her feet
On the clothes line
And the ground she stood on.

300 million volts
Preparing a bolt
"Do not stand under a tree during a storm"
"Keep your feet together in a storm"
"The safest place to hide in a storm is a vehicle"
Too little too late

They were there
300 million volts

SOLITARY CONFINEMENT

I live in solitary confinement
A prison made of layers upon layers of assumptions
Reinforced by my belief systems
Traditions
Truisms
Rituals
All wrapped up under my skin

From the day I was born
I began building walls
My mother loved me as her son
Wrapped me up in a certain way
Different than Joe Sop
Thereby creating the first difference
Laying foundations for my confinement
Thereafter wall building I did subconsciously.

As I grew older I thought my wall was thinner than the next kid
And sought to make it even thicker.
My siblings lovingly fought me
Creating layers of walls
My education taught me the right way
And supposedly the wrong way
Adding to my confinement
Today I am always looking for the right way
And most times blinker away from the real way.

The Boys Brigade
The Boy Scouts

Heaping convention upon rigid convention
Erecting walls
In religious halls
I am good if I did this
Rude if I did that
Reinforcing my prison walls

And now I wonder if it's not too late to breakout
To transcend
Pull these unnecessary walls down
The paradox is, am I not creating new cells?
Fighting my confinement?
Is it even there?
And not just a figment of my imagination
Something I feel but never feel to touch

To be fair
There is peace in solitary confinement
Where I am me, myself and I
The only master of my soul and spirit
The only wearer of my skin
But, alas, I have missed so many trains
Stuck in solitary confinement
My solitary confinement.

QUENCHING OBSESSIONS

My thoughts are about you
with you
for you
Wherever
and whenever

It seems empty space can only exist in the mind in meditation
but only for those able to close the aperture of their consciousness
In meditation, the opening to my consciousness is clogged by acute desire for you.

Nights are fitfully occupied by nightmares of the day
Thoughts that death, sickness and infirmity can become your reality are imprinted on my mind in your absence
In my sleep, I get love sick having virtual dreams of you unwell
while I drown in rivulets of unrequited love

Quarantine is no panacea either
There is no guarantee there is safety in quarantine
Invisible pestilence colonizing every space wherever you are
And, in quarantine the threat of sleep apnoea caused by irregular respiration gives me no rest at all,
afraid, in your absence I may stop breathing

If I can't be with you in the binary of our love
I am grudgingly in acceptance of only harbouring thoughts

of you
But, where can we quell these urges?

The solution is to have you next to me
In meditation
In bed
Even in quarantine
Quenching obsessions

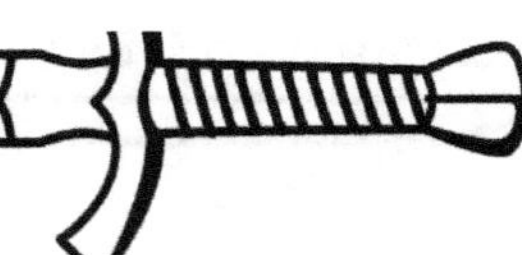

SOMEONE CARES

In my domain of solitude
Where sorrows grow
Worries congeal
Like sacrificial blood
Where tears flow to dry up
Leaving scars down my cheeks
I hear whispers of encouragement
I feel life giving lips
Breathing into my heart
And I feel the soft pressure
On my chest keeping me breathing
I feel wanted
Cared for
Encouraged
Renewed
Someone cares.

The lumber I bear
Digging deep in my shoulder
Drawing blood
The fake tiara
Pricking life out of my head
And the slope to the hill
Made steeper by the whip
Are no match for the love
Of the invisible
I bear them with a smile
Knowing next to me
Someone heals
Soothes

I can take it
I can make it
Someone cares.

WAR IN UKRAINE

I don't understand human beings
The double standards in our dealings
I sympathise with the people of Ukraine
But, wish everyone had had the same refrain

NATO bombed Libya
It's obvious because they were seen as an inferior race
There was deafening silence
Loud cheering acceptance

Based on lies Iraqi was bombed
the whole Middle East mobbed
The list of countries destroyed by the West
fills a whole encyclopaedia at worst.

Whether you like what I say or not
The truth never aborts
Russia and Ukraine are neighbours
and have been since time immemorial

Their misunderstanding is engineered by enemies of peace
hegemonies tearing them to pieces
for ideological pleasure
ignoring the mortal dangers

Instigating a brutal tribal war
For, you must know,
that's what the war would have been called
had two neighbouring African states been involved.

I hope the war in Ukraine ends soon
I also hope poets can be truthful about doom and gloom
wherever it happens
whoever it happens to
for karma is non-racial
because no one is special

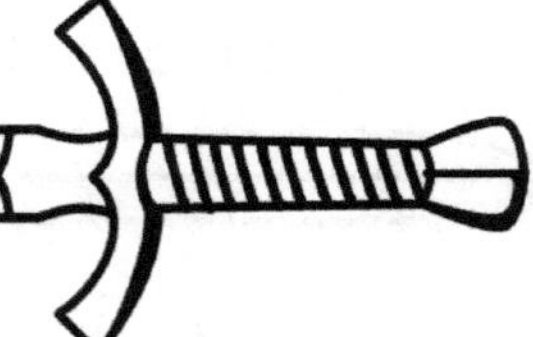

MY FIELD OF VIEW

I was sitting on a brown leather sofa in my lounge
In front of me on the ceramic floor tile, an Asian carpet
A black carpet with motifs of African Savannah big five animals
An elephant, a lion, buffalo, rhinoceros and a leopard
On top of the carpet a small side table 500mm square
Looking straight ahead, the corner of another leather seat
on the opposite side of where I was sitting

Beyond that, a lone dining room chair
and a picture of a girl on the wall
My son's beautiful art
After that the doorway to the kitchen
And a loose upright kitchen cabinet
I wanted to refurbish that soon and mount it in its final position
Someday soon when I can take time off from writing poetry
In the kitchen there were black ceramic tiles on the floor

My flip flops were just inside the entrance to the kitchen
I was thinking how dangerous it was to leave shoes inside the doorway
Someone may trip entering the kitchen
Oh well!
The lower stable door of my kitchen was closed
The top open
Beyond the kitchen door I could see clothes
Clothes swaying in the wind pinned on the wire line with wooden pegs
Beyond the line my boundary wall

Green creepers adorned my wall
On the other property was a cottage
Prominent on its side a toilet vent pipe pointing skywards
And beyond the cottage the main house

After the main house, a tree with light green leaves
Then another further on with darker green leaves waving in the wind
In the distance grey white clouds
Now and then a voyeur of sexy blue skies in the chink of the clouds.
There were things I couldn't see
Things I knew where there regardless
I knew beyond the clouds and blue skies were stars and planets
Possibly even earth satellites lurking in near earth orbit.

I knew there were galaxies in my field of view
Not able to be seen with my naked eyes
But, they were there all the same
I knew there were black holes
Dark energy
Comets
And asteroids
Pity I couldn't see them
In my field of view

LONG LIVE THE POEM

If a poet writes a poem
does the poem become the poet?
Is the poet the poem?

Often times some read me in my poems
instead of reading the poem in me
to the extent some dislike the messenger
disregarding the message

Are we the same?

What a poet writes is the sum total of his experiences
an extension of one's consciousness
but, there are poems people write as animals
even as dead people
it cannot wholly be true
that a poet is the poem

I have conversations with the sun
the moon
the stars
but, I am not crazy
I think I am not
Why would you, then, hate me for the rantings of my poet-
ry?
I am not the poem

I may have birthed it
but a poem takes a life of its own once its born
That is why it must be unrestrained

constrained by a person's locus of misunderstanding
a person's span of experience

I have been on poetry fora
To my horror
My poems were taken as me
sanctioned
as if freedom to be is a preserve of some
and not others.

Sometimes, I consciously have a topic
a message to impart in a poem
the poem refuses my topic and ideas
A new poem emerges with a different theme
because a poem is not me
and I am not the poem

When a mother gives birth to a child
the child is a separate person
after breastfeeding,
sending to school
and coming of age
you can't blame the mother for the behaviour of the child

This is why two people reading a poem may interpret it
differently depending on plenty factors
experience
disposition
prejudices
preferences
ignorance
depth

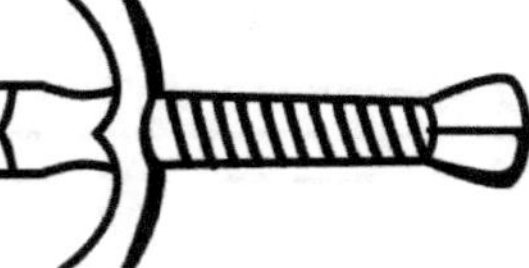

literacy

Let that poem live
I am not the poem
The poem is not me
I am me
and long live the poem

IN THE KNOW

Doctors are supposed to be your friends
The contradictions are glaring
They can be the bearer of the worst news
When they look you straight in the eye
To tell you that you are terminal
Some of them seem to have developed a side effect
A sadistic tendency to smile when they drop the bomb
Perhaps in my imagination
It's like the dry humour I meet at police stations
There in the charge office is a sticker written in bold
"Police are your friend"
Really?
Every time I have been at the police stations I was roughed up
Traumatised even.

So, I am at the neurosurgeon
An MRI was done to my brain, neck and back
And I have come for my review
Doctors are supposed to be your friends
So I hope if the news is bad, he will be friendly enough to let me know
It's better to be in the know
Than not to know
Whatever happens the poems will write themselves.

A STRONG AND BEAUTIFUL FOSSIL

I lived on the edge of reality
driving my body to extremes
drowning in both alcohol
and vain fitness convolutions

Balanced diets were for sissies
sufficient sleep the luxury of lazy bums
never worried about the toll on my body
like a perpetual motion human machine
trying to squeeze every iota of existence
out of existence

Now in my sixties it's payback time
My aging mortal frame I have to boost
I do 5 kilometre brisk walking
watch the carbs I eat
drink water to a minimum of two litres a day
have adequate sleep

I am getting stronger
getting healthier with stronger stamina and bones
all soon to be buried six feet in the ground
as a strong and beautiful fossil

POETRY VALLEY

Even though I walk in this valley of poetics
I fear I will never make it to my destination.
That place of peace
The valley of poetry being endless,
ideas ageless
This particular journey for one,
is a one way ticket to silence

In this valley I move among mysterious forms
Wondering where all these passages lead
whether following them
leads to new revelations
of peace in time
or a time in peace
a time at which peace becomes timeless.
and poetry ends in a perfect cadence,
at the end of time

There are so many ways in the valley
to express the passage of time
with not every alley leading to epiphany
For, that's what I think I seek
I seek a point where words are so valuable
their meaning priceless,
their rhythms timeless

Many have gone on epic journeys through the valley of poetry,
the timelessness of their fossils is now questionable
their endeavours reading hollow as time approaches space

So, I ask myself if ever I shall reach that settlement
where poetry speaks all languages,
never lost in translation,
never lost in interpretation

I wonder, though, as I wander,
whether it is not time to face reality,
turn back and explain it was a mistake
For, how will I survive in the valley of poetry
being so poorly equipped
I have not read the maps sufficiently
and my tools are not suited, will never be suitable for easy
wayfaring.
I do not even have reference books and guides and am left
to fumble in the dark,
deriving survival skills from first principles

Shall I turn back now?
Is there a way out of the labyrinth?
Perhaps or perhaps not.
It might be time to accept that I will never make it,
that, it is time to continue wandering in the valley of poet-
ry,
leaving markers on the way
Those foolish enough to follow shall, one day, stumble up-
on the skeleton of my poesy,
dead in the poetry valley.

HORNS

Each party claims their horn is the biggest
the loudest

To some, the horns sound like music
To others it makes them sick

and yet both noises have impurities
deliberately detuned to confuse

Those who refuse to listen are
subjected to ridicule
Within the harmonics is the hidden message

"Our way or the highway"
"You are either with us or you are a target"

depriving discourse for a middle ground.

Each side has powerful amplifiers
with unbridled root mean square power
so much so that the repeat button becomes worn more
than the horn
trying to win the hearts and minds of people caught in the
melee.
No one wants to back down
Unfortunately for innocent bystanders
the horns can lock to disastrous consequences
because no one is listening.

NUCLEAR DIPLOMACY

When talking is considered nonsense
mandibles rendered useless
a new way for discourse
becomes brute force

Even inviting your nemesis for tea
to make the opposing view seen
is seen as a waste of time
akin to an ideological crime

preferring grave sabre rattling
leading to battling.
Those who live in glass houses
must never stone grouses

Some of the missiles
maybe fissile
leading to nuclear despondency
instead of new clear diplomacy

which is sitting down
hankering down
writing down
bowing down

Listening
listing
talking
noting

Nuclear war
Is a no no
Nuclear diplomacy
No substitute for new clear diplomacy

THE "I'

The "I" in my poetry stems from the eye
What I see in my day to day living
Giving the false impression of not giving
Others a chance
That my life is a solo dance
That it is all about me
All about "I'

I am not saying I am not there
Let's be fair
I am outnumbered one to eight billion
Counting the number of people
And this is a trickle
If I were to compare with everything under the sun
And infinity if I included the universe just for fun

Forgive me if you find my poems only about me
About "I"
I won't lie
Most of what I write is about my experiences
Excuse me
Where I fault myself is when I write as if I exist alone
I have to atone

I have to write from a different perspective
Be reflective
Give voice to the voiceless
Even the noiseless
The rocks and all things inanimate
Not only primates

Finding a voice in me
In the "I"

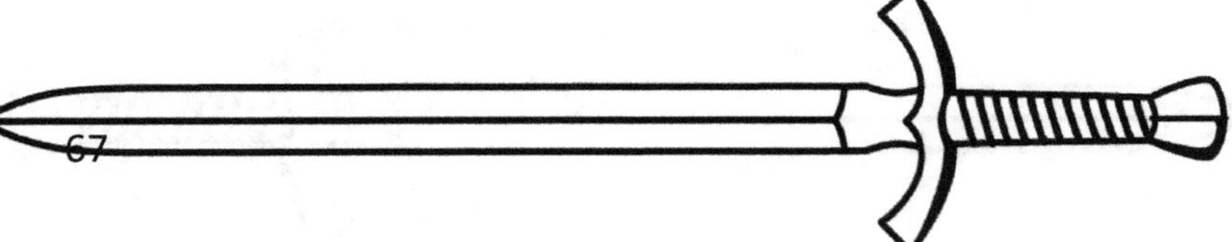

SHONA SADZA STANZA

I am truly thankful for flora and fauna
Flora speaks to me in Shona
The tongue of my forebearers
Whose palettes imbibed opaque beers
Brewed from choice seeds and yeast
Sadza providing a feast.
Colonist English cucumber
Speaking deliciously in a starter

Fauna depended on species
Animated speeches
Barking dogs
Oinking hogs
Feline purrs
Birds of prey
Cows mooing
Doves cooing

To my utter surprise
Humans abandoned me
To the extent I sought communion hugging trees
Whispering to dogs and cats feeling free
My blood brother forsaking our brotherhood
Influenced by in-laws up to no good.
Friends boycotting
Leaving me frothing and coughing

There was no one
I did what had to be done
Embracing flora and fauna

Speaking to me in floral Shona
Flora giving soda
Energy to write a stanza
English cucucucucumber
Speaking with a stutter.

CIRCUMSTANCES

Circumstances viewed from a distance,
are at that instance,
consistent with the persistent opinion existent at that juncture,
but in no way represent the present facts presented by evidence at hand.

Circumstance is a transient happenstance with minimal substance and one is ill advised to form substantial decisions on the subsistence of evidence gleaned from such chance observations.

Many carry prejudices, foreclosed positions, and manufactured consent to disastrous consequences due to wanton disregard for empiricism.

JOHNNIE WALKER

Fads are two a penny
Dads a rare breed
My father gave me life lessons
No quibbling
Matter of fact
Sometimes lacking tact

I miss his ways
These days
It's all about do this
If you want bliss
All to do with marketing
Making money
It's no longer funny

Some advice is contradictory
Even conflicting
Coffee being good and bad
Caffeine making you sad.
Quite refreshing
Quite depressing

I took a 5 kilometre walk
My therapist sneaking it in during his talk
I walked past a heap of rubbish
There was a bottle of Johnnie Walker
Alcohol good for the mood
Bad for the heart once you start

I felt like a stalker more than a walker.

Being the talker after a bottle of Johnnie Walker
Good is bad
Mood became sad.
Walking is good
"Johnnie Walker" just being rude

WITHOUT A MIND

I see strange things in this world
Things about which I have no words
Like the human spirit has finally failed

There is a rush for misguided superiority
Hypersonic and unbridled lethality
Shrouding our earth with mushrooms of uncertainty

Me thinks some people are aliens
Their urge to go back home endless
Leaving aboriginal sapiens homeless

Taking off on spaceships to go back home
Earth written off as a bygone
To be fossilised with billions of human bones

Otherwise how do we explain the lack of global leadership
The belligerent brinkmanship
Launch upon launch of spaceships

Money wasted on killing machines instead of healing
Mother earth reduced to comorbidities of killings
Rifts 'tween east and west festering without humane feel-
ings

I see these things in this world
Things about which I have no real words
Like the human spirit has finally been unfurled

Run aground
Wondering round and round
Without a mind.

BILLOWING SMOKE

Billowing smoke rises up and up
like an apparition
casting a hazy shadow on the ground

It is the final solution

One man decides to expire another
with or without justification
with or without provocation

In spite of there being other means and methods of con-
flict resolution
he packages the lack of tolerance in incendiary

The billowing smoke is the harbinger of a revolution
a change by force
I am yet to fathom why man subjugates another
why the myriad ideas cannot coexist

why they cannot mingle and evolve forever
together
why extremes have to be meted out on one by another
taking the role of the creator

when,
at the end of the day the billowing smoke
carrying the dreams and aspiration of the deceased
may, one day, billow for all.

THAT DAY

One day I shall wake up without the world
Or, rather the world without me
Having moved on to nether lands
Free of the prejudices of man
Where equality is at atomic level
Not some arbitrary label

I shall have shed off the albatross of my identity
The colour of my skin
My ethnicity
Electricity will be electrons going round my nuclei
My global positioning coordinates
Never the property of any government

There I shall make my most valued contribution
A free elemental form so critical to the health of the cos-
mos
Vibrating to infinity without contrition
Without conditions
Unlike now where everything I do is judged
Conditional upon satisfying someone or something.

One day I shall wake up without the world
Or, rather the world without me
I know the sun will not bate an eyelid
The moon will never wink
Only the earth will turn inside out for me
That Day

PRAY PREY

The beast is tiring
Running out of steam
Not out of carrion
Just boredom
Having the same meal
In the carnage
Of human flesh and blood

Even as it tires
It's seven canines sharp as ever
Hard at work
Ripping up the world.
The sharpest impaling hapless bodies
The second dripping blue blood
The third savouring dark meat
The fourth eastern cuisine

The fifth, sixth and seventh ready for new recipes
Of human beings
Of fleshy things.
It's metabolism slowing
Signs of hibernation showing
In just over a month the beast will tire
And sleep at the edge of horror

The edge of horror just a mirror
A portal to new suffering
For humanity
The beast having gone round the world
Eating.

Feasting on the seven tribes
As foretold long ago

Even as the beast tires
And prepares to sleep at the edge of horror
Beyond the darkness lies another
Fresh, hungry and ready to start feeding
Those bipeds that make it out of this quagmire
Fall from the stewing pot into the fire.
Crying and begging for quick death.

On the last day of December twenty twenty one
The new terror in the dark will open its eyes,
It's ravenous mouth
And partake of those who made it beyond.
Behold
The deaths will continue
Unabated

So pray
Pray Prey
Pray.
Pray for vaccination
Inoculation
From the beast of prey
And beat the east beast.

POEM HUNGER

It's like my stomach is in my head
The hunger for a poem
stimulating my artistic senses
to the extent
on a full stomach
I would rather break my fast with verses
ignoring the dieticians advice for veggies

At lunch I would rather recite ballads
skipping the bowl of salads
and supping only after writing a poem
any excuse to forego the porridge.

Poem hunger is the starter that primes my craving for food
The best way to buoy my mood
Reading a good poem is like smoking a good joint
my dopamine levels at optimum levels
writing one even better
in the verse, enjoying the sound of every letter
to the extent sometimes I giggle with pleasure
Those alone moments totally treasured

And, unlike the satiety of food
poem hunger will never bloat
distend the brain
or, cause a brain clot
Give me a poem anytime
it doesn't have to rhyme
as long as it satisfies my poem hunger.

RACIST THOUGHTS

1. The BBC

"It's very emotional for me because I see European people with blue eyes and blonde hair being killed" - Ukraine's Deputy Chief Prosecutor, David Sakvarelidze

2. CBS News

"This isn't Iraq or Afghanistan...This is a relatively civilized, relatively European city" - CBS foreign correspondent Charlie D'Agata

3. Al-Jazeera

"What's compelling is looking at them, the way they are dressed. These are prosperous, middle-class people. These are not obviously refugees trying to get away from the Middle East...or North Africa. They look like any European family that you'd live next door to."

4. BFM TV (France)

"We are in the 21st century, we are in a European city and we have cruise missile fire as though we were in Iraq or Afghanistan, can you imagine!?"

5. The Daily Telegraph

This time, war is wrong because the people look like us and have Instagram and Netflix accounts. It's not in a poor, remote country any more. - Daniel Hannan

6. ITV (UK)

"The unthinkable has happened...This is not a developing, third world nation; this is Europe!"

7. BFM TV (France)

"It's an important question. We’re not talking here about Syrians fleeing...We're talking about Europeans."

8. "To put it bluntly, these are not refugees from Syria, these are refugees from Ukraine...They're Christians, they're white. They're very similar [to us]" - explaining why Poland is accepting refugees.

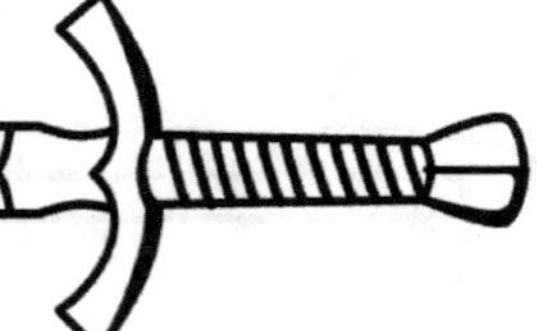

POINT BLANK BLACK

Racists think black people are inferior
By inference they are superior
When research is done
Truth is we are just but one
People migrated out of Africa
Out of Sudan going right up to Antarctica
It is the African genome and it's robustness
Mixed with Neanderthals in their remoteness
Which saved the world from extinction
The African genome has distinction.
Look at Covid statistics
The death rate of black people in Africa is fantastic

Being black doesn't mean I lack
Like a flower I have the power
To outshine the brightest
The colour you see on me
Is a skin so thin
Evolution devolution
Millions of years of having fun in the sun
Producing calciferol more that calcium
Vitamin D produced for free
More melanin than Melania
Tell that fair Hungarian Aryan
Being African doesn't mean I cannot.

MY POEMS

Most of my me time is taken up by poetry
An observer sees me typing on my cell phone
Assumes I am having a quiet moment
And, fortunately, mostly reserve their comments
I am not alone
Even at home
I am at work
With words

I am talking with many words
All aloof
Trying to make them line up correctly
Speak to me correctly
Phonetically
Metaphorically
And this is easier conceived than done
Let alone easier said than done

I am seldom happy with words talking back at me
Not the kind of talking back which gives positive feedback
The kind that tells you the words are on strike
Refusing, not in so many words, to do what you like
After a few lines you realise words are not your only problem
You African wannabe poet of limited vocabulary
The syntax, grammar, spelling and most tellingly the prosody
They are just not there, it's not fair

Fortunately my hard Shona type psychic does not accept

defeat
I sit there during my me time
Without a dictionary
Sans thesaurus
And joust with the Queen's language until it happens
I feel a tingling sensation in my eyes
And then I know somehow my words evoke an emotion
I know someone out there will feel some of what I feel

What I feel is real
And I hope it comes out in the verses
Adjectives and adverbs
Images and metaphors
Crude poetic devices
The rhyming or lack thereof
Of my poems
And the way they are arranged

SOMETHING IS WRONG

How things have changed
The sun used to give specific instructions
The wind dutifully obeying
shooing moisture laden hot gusts of wind to the strato-
sphere

Dry air falling to the ground in a dance so familiar
Born of this cyclic waltz dark pregnant cumulonimbus
clouds
shedding tears punctuated by flashes of intense lightning
and peals of deep sadistic laughter

We were never fazed
We would dig holes and bury a seed
knowing by 15 October our wet dream would come
The sky would scream in agony
birthing life
waters breaking to our sheer delight.

October last
The sun dutifully gave specific instructions
So we thought
Temperatures off the scale
Nothing happened
November came and went
So did December
Beginning January the clouds wept
The farmer wept too

The seed he planted died in the womb of the earth

No life giving water
He replanted
The skies wouldn't give
Then in the fortuitous month of January
the sky obeyed the sun and rained
daily for 31days
And on the last day of January the heavens switched off
the taps
Crops cried for more rain but it was
turned off
Gone

The sun used to give specific instructions
The wind dutifully obeying
shooing moisture laden hot gusts of wind to the strato-
sphere
Not anymore
It's all gone
Something is wrong.

HA HA HA HAA

They come across funny
Finding humour in things absurd

Nothing they do, they do not jest about
Inside and out

They do racial jokes
Belittle other folks

They can be sexist
even Marxist

Joke about nuclear war
The suffering of survivors even more

The more people laugh
the more they feel tough
to the extent reality and humour blend
going round the bend
as if drunk on nitrogen
Or, overdosed on nitrous oxide
laughing offside

By the time they realise the jokes are stale
There is a story to tell
The only people laughing
Ha ha ha haa!!!
being comedians

PIXELATED PERFECTION

It is no longer true
In reality
That the beautiful ones are not yet born
They were finally born
one dot at a time
digitised in mega pixels
1920 by 1080 resolution
getting better with digital revolution.

Every dot perfectly in place
accentuating the face
make up covering pimples
exposing sensual dimples
She's every woman
. in perfect poise
Controlled lighting
making her exciting

They are finally born
on the big screen
Every man drooling
Perfect face
curves in the right place
silicon bust
small waist
accentuated behinds

Flaunting wealth

on reality shows
bling bling bringing more cash
dressed in Kaleidoscopes of Khaki
And Kinky Jewels
the rest being good lighting
And a matrix of dots
For Pixelated Perfection.

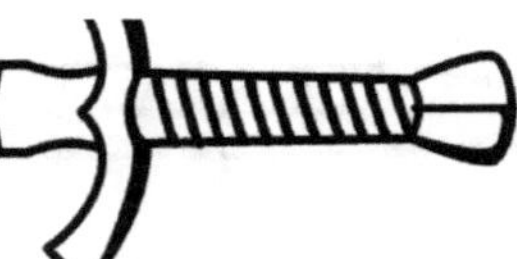

LIVING AND LET LIVING

As the second hand chases the minute hand chasing the hour hand
I try to synchronise my doings with their animation
Only to realise ulcers occasioned by hyper acidity is the usual reward
Sometimes I ride the tip of the hour hand
Every time it ticks I am tricked into complacency
thinking I have it in sync with my aspiration
only to find out my biological clock resists such synchrony

The hour hand cannot and will not be in harmony with my needs
and so I step down to the minute hand
Conservatively riding the centre of its beam
Every minute, every commitment needing a second attempt
I am in contempt of every rule
Every minute committing mean culpa
to the extent no one with a right mind gives me a second chance
I shall not speak of the second hand as
all my efforts are second hand
It seems the way out is never to
mind the second hand chasing the minute hand chasing the hour hand
understanding life is too short chasing chronological impossibilities
Living and let living is the best motto

TWO SCORE YEARS

This month two score years ago
A teenage girl of fifteen took a risk
Met an eighteen year old young man
Fell headlong
Being head strong
In love
They told her be careful
That she was too young
Still in school
It wasn't cool
Eight years later they were married
Still married today
Two score years later
Happy 40th anniversary, Barbara
I promised to take you to an island
Just for the two of us
Now our kids are grown
Gone
We live alone
In our home
An island
Keep holding my hand
And love me

TILL KINGDOM COME

(Dedicated to my wife and queen of 40 years and counting).

The End Without A Bend

The journey I have been travelling is unravelling
coming to an end without a bend
The stops I intended to drop off a sermon non-existent
There is a brush where the bus was to stop
The deity I have been exhorting dirty and cold
the seed he needs to appease my "Please!"
I am told he wants it only in gold
I feel no less than a tired coward
A teacher who is also a cheater
Teaching and preaching from the book of doom
To my left I felt like I spoke with a cleft lip
To the right like I fight for the rights of the right-wing
Whatever I said I am afraid was lost at my cost
My speech rolling off a forked tongue with double-speak
In my mind doom and gloom loomed
mired in double trouble all the way.
the journey I have been travelling unravelling
reaching the journey's end
The end without a bend

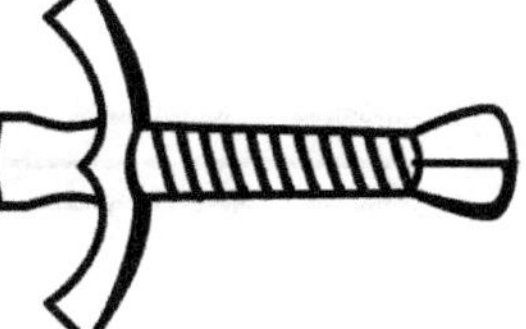

NO MORE

Those who promised me pies in the sky
The time is up to fulfil your promises
I want them pies
All twenty one types of them

The mountains they promised to move for me
I want to ascend to the summit
As they say the higher you go the cooler it becomes
I want to look and feel cool at the apex.

Those who promised me heaven and earth
I am ready to ascend the golden stairs
To go where no one goes alive
and still come back to claim the earth.

Those who promised me the earth
Let me have real estate here on this earth
From Africa to the Americas
The Middle East, the Near and Far East

Many stand in front of me
Without irony
Utter words devoid of substance
Taking me for a ride
Give me the ride
No more metaphors

GONE TO THE DOGS

My Maltese, Ziggy, died
He just went under my car and expired
Flossy, the bitch, cried
Was very unhappy, looking tired

These little mutts are intelligent
Showing emotions just like you and I
And they are also quite diligent
Barking only when necessary at night.

When Ziggy passed on
Flossy became totally withdrawn
Stopped playing and eating on her own
We thought she was also going

Later, we found out it was depression
Like any human would feel
Showing sadness in expression
Ziggy's death to Flossy was a big deal

I see people killing each other
Without even as much as flinching
Murdering own ethnic brother
Like during slavery, lynching

And, I think to myself in retrospect
Humans have gone to the dogs
Having not even an iota of respect
To similar creations of God

PREVENTION AND CURE

Prevention is not always better than cure
unless your heart is pure
because you can never be sure sure
your opponent will be demure.

Many times you agonize
trying to strategize
how to apologize
all you do is antagonize

The strife you wanted to prevent
becoming an explosive event
when someone vents
causing an even bigger dent

I LIKE THAT

I have been fortunate to meet many caricatures of man
been unfortunate with some
fortunate with others
Man including woman
I do not know why
Sigh!
Not all resonated with me

My race
My face

I met some whose eyes lit up in the presence of women
Some whose feet faced the opposite of where we went
Others whose template was intemperate
Breathing fire all the time
Even under liquid conditions
Funny how they chased after money

All in all
I befriended the tall
The short
Fascists
Racists
and snobs
Beauties and beasts
And thought I had seen it all
Till I found myself
Overtime

I have come to morph into who I am today

I have to say
I don't know how
I did not start this way
I suspect it's the thugs I hugged
the ones I shoved
and the ones I loved

I cannot brag
that I have got it in the bag
Only that I am free
Freer
In my career
Careering in freefall
To a singularity
a peculiarity
a personality
and I like that

A SEA WITHOUT FISH

Loneliness is a sea without fish
fish having evolved growing legs
emptying the liquid firmament
ambling out beyond the shore
forgetting the ambience of water
and abandoning a fisherman whose totem is the fish

First swimming up and landing,
The Whale
followed closely by shoals of cold blooded cousins
plankton crossing the plank last
fast leaving a man with a fishing rod
unaware the sea is depleted
emptied of sustenance

A soul whose reflection is shrouded in loneliness
whose silhouette against the sea
causes him not to see
the diminished sustenance
leaving a profound void
a loud silence
and the realisation
loneliness is a sea without fish

LOVE IS.......

Fungible and tangible
that's what love is
stored in the heart
or the mind
swapped for affection
or fondness
and still having the power
to grow things all over the world
It can evoke happiness
but, also clothe the world in sadness

Love can impart joy to a boy
and gaily to a girl
bringing forth harmony in matrimony
It can beget relief with a bit of belief
for a brief period grief if you don't believe
It can be empty in the fullness of time
full of empty promises punctuated by cries in crisis
It tends to pretend when forged by force
but may be easygoing by eloping,
like the gentle slope of a natural incline

Love can cause swooning in a looming ballooning
or an elevation of elation during inflation
though at other times,
bleeding leading to complications with implications
Realising you spawned your own in the deed you did
you wander wondering what love is.
Love is what it is
but, never ask what it is

because love is none of the above
it is everything for everyone
fungible and tangible

IN A VERSE

The one whose lonely moments
are flooded with comments
has nothing to say
today
mind distracted
ideas diffracted

The one whose lips cannot land a fly
no matter how it tries
always having a say
today
silent
like a remote island

Thoughts are panicked dwellers
like stadium revellers
exiting at once
calling nine one one
gate too small
for all

Words locked in the mouth
not coming out
like prisoners
with listeners
afraid to be quoted
and noted

What to do for a scribe
to try to describe

what's on the mind
and behind the bind
except in verbs
in verses

A HAPPY NATIVE

Today I was fortunate
the heavy rains of the past two weeks had subsided
I took in the sites and scenes
of this my beautiful homeland
as my little Honda ate the miles
I couldn't help but smile

Trees lined up on both sides of the road
seemingly standing to attention
saluting me
some joyfully waving in the wind at my car
while my car caressed the warm tar

Even the long queue at the toll booth
could not spoil my mood
I even exchanged pleasantries with the revenue officer
said, hie de hie
though I won't lie
The two dollars toll
is not fair at all

From there the euphoria reached fever pitch
Everyone in high spirits
even goats I met at the turn off to my plot
bleating happily a lot
my workers joyful
giving me a very short list of problems
and a lot of farm produce

My little Honda groaned under
bundles of green veggies
fresh corn
and sweet potatoes
and like the little sweet chariot she is
carried me back home
a happy native

DOUBLE EDGED WORDS

I am the one whose world is made of words
every stanza written is a bonanza gathering ideas and
thoughts taught and or not taught
though, most may come to nought

I am the one condemned and code named
the Joe Doe they don't want to know
eternally interred in frozen contextually contrived words
buried on the fringe of a frigid world

By reason of eccentricity of my ethnicity
weird words are wielded
and attributed to force majeure
generously generated to generalise
fictional stereotypical biases laced with aliases
painting a faint caricature of Kunta Kinte
far far below par in the spectral bar

My anatomy is generally generic
the devious deviation from the mean only seen through
diffraction gratings of hate
words used to abuse the observed triviality of inequality
volumes of fiction causing friction
through huge transmitters seemingly beaming messages
with copious draughts of negative innuendos

I am the one whose world is made of words
for whom actuality in reality
is a stanza gathering ideas
thoughts taught and or not taught

whose double edged words in this world
taunt and haunt me no end

FREE SPACE POETICA

Some attended poetry school
that is totally cool
except most become preoccupied with form
possibly because they wore uniform

It is important to study form in poetry
Just as it is free range chicken in poultry
though at the nutritional level
the stomach forgets the labels

A poem reads good
not because of form but mood
but, if you have to judge poems correctly
it has to be regulated phonetically
that is understood
and very good

Shakespeare was good
I hope I am not rude
but I would be a fool
a real shrew
trying to wear his shoes
because we have different views

Lamentations were different
by inference
our ways of speech
the way we speak
our experiences

differentiates expressions

Those who dote on Shakespeare
do not come at me with a spear
I write in peace
please
unchain poetry
like free range poultry
because even the definition of it
is controversial quite a bit

When a good poem is read
It rings good in your head
touching the heart
beating it apart
maintaining your sanity
in sanctity
so, at this stage
free space poetica

ABOUT ME

I was born on June 18, 1964 in Southern Zimbabwe, in a village called Davira in Chivi District, Masvingo Province.

I am a professional electrical engineer; a product of the University of Zimbabwe. Poetry, though, is my passion. I have published seven books so far, six of which are available on Amazon and Kindle. My seventh book: "Mbiresaurus" was self-publish as part of the learning process. This one is the eighth.

I hope to keep writing poetry, keep improving my craft and publish more books.

Deluke Muwanigwa. C. 2023